LIFE
LESSONS for WOMEN

By Cindy Francis

Newport House, Inc.

Newport House, Inc.
107 R.R. 620 S.,
Suite 7-A
Austin, TX 78734

Life Lessons for Women/ Cindy Francis
First Newport House edition, 1992

Design and typeset by Barbara Jezek
Cover illlustration by Marie Zimmerman

Manufactured in the United States of America

ISBN O-939515-46-6

INTRODUCTION

This book was written for a young woman named Anna, who is one of my best friends. Anna comes by to visit often, and we talk about our families, friends, business, tennis, and how to get along in the world. When Anna has a problem, I often find I've faced something similar myself—and have learned a lesson which is useful to her.

One day, feeling very ambitious, I decided to put together a book for Anna made up of my life lessons. As I was preparing the book, I asked many women I respect to share their thoughts, and some of those are in the book as well.

That little book for Anna has become the one you're reading right now. It's full of big and small life lessons. Some were learned with joy and some with much pain. Some were easy to accept and some quite difficult. But all have added a measure of pleasure, success, and ease to my life and to the lives of other women. My hope is that you will find these lessons of value.

Look for the positive.

Ask for help when
you need it.

Celebrate your victories,
however small.

Enjoy what you have.

Finish what you start.

Hold on to your dreams.

Keep your promises.

Buy quality.

Keep in touch
with old friends.

Let your enthusiasm show.

Admit when
you're wrong.

Reward yourself often—
You deserve it!

Show up early.

Sit in the front row.

If you're there,
be *there*.

Whistle when you're happy.

When you want advice,
ask someone who's
done it successfully.

Shower those you care for
with genuine praise.

Speak up!
People can't read your mind.

Have ice cream with everything
on it once in a while.

Give *more*
than is expected.

Do your best with
what you've got.

Let go of things you
can't have anyway.

Take time to exercise.

If you're too busy
to have fun,
you're too busy.

Read every day.

Think long-term.

Spend less than you
earn and save the rest.

Separate your needs
from your wants.

Do something each day that makes
you happy. If you don't know
what makes you happy, do things
that used to make you happy.

Find a hobby.

Be curious.

Write someone you love
a note saying so.

Even though you've been hurt,
keep your heart open.

Happiness starts with you.

Recycle, even if
it's less convenient.

View *all* your feelings as acceptable.

You don't have to
always be right.

Assume that if *you* don't do it, it won't get done.

When someone hurts you, let them know right away.

Say yes only to requests you have time for.

Always treat your body with respect.

If you want to get better, practice.

Act like a winner and you're well on your way to being a winner.

You are never really stuck.
There is always *something*
you can do.

Let go of friendships that hold you
back from growing and succeeding.

Drop all "musts",
"shoulds", and "oughts."

Limit TV to 1 hour a day or less.

Do today's work today.
It won't be any easier tomorrow.

Think before you speak.

Break down big challenges
into little pieces.
Then do them one by one.

Put your goals in writing.

When you feel sad, realize that
it's temporary.

Surprise friends with little gifts.

Take a weekend off and go traveling with a friend.

Encourage others to talk about themselves. They'll think *you're* a brilliant conversationalist.

Teach others by setting a good example.

Never sacrifice your health
for any other advantage.

Balance your life between time spent
alone and time spent with others.

Take yoga classes.

Have 15 minutes of quiet time a day.

Think of "love" as a verb.
It's not something to have and
ignore, but something to work at.

Set aside money to use
only for having fun.

Get out in nature each day.

Start a "Victory" journal and write down every success you have.

Call people by name when you speak with them.

Make friends with successful people. You become like those you spend time with.

Keep learning.

Read *Conversationally Speaking* to learn skills for relating better with people.

Network. What you know is important, but *who* you know is often more important.

Admit the truth, at least to yourself.

You have the right to say "No" without feeling guilty.

Ask for what you want.

Whatever you do, either get all the way in or all the way out.

Have lots of celebrations.

Make a list of what you admire about someone. Work at bringing those virtues to your own life.

Give more than you take.

Don't waste time feeling sorry for yourself.

Get the facts first. Most problems aren't so hard to solve once you fully understand them.

Give your old clothes to the Salvation Army.

To persuade others, give them a reason why it is in *their* interest to do what you want them to do.

Recognize that everyone is doing their best as they see it.

Never invest in anything you don't completely understand.

Never invest in coins, precious metals or the futures markets, even if you think you understand them.

If you can't change the situation, change your *attitude* towards it.

Take long bubble baths.

Make decisions by listing the
PROS and CONS down on a
sheet and then weighing them.

Don't quit at the first sign
of problems. Or the second.

Write down ideas as
you think of them.

If you have a choice between
being loved or being right,
choose to be loved.

Listen to what your body tells you.

Find things to be
happy about.

When you make a mistake, ask yourself, "When I'm 70, will this really matter?"

It's important for you to take care of yourself *first* sometimes.

Criticism of you isn't the truth— it's just someone's opinion.

Get together with friends and brainstorm new ideas and solutions to problems.

Take time for spiritual growth.

Trust most those who have earned your trust.

Find a cause to work for.

Consider mistakes nothing more than detours on the way to success. Learn from them, and then go on.

Compliment *yourself* several times a day.

Try new recipes.

When you're worried, ask yourself,
"How likely is that really to happen?"
Most often the things we worry about
are not at all likely.

Don't waste time
regretting the past.

Let go of super-high standards for yourself and others. You *can* be happy in an imperfect world.

Compliment the cook.

Enjoy each moment as it happens. Your life is made up of one moment after another, either lived or lost.

Get started—and you've already jumped the highest hurdle in most tasks.

Visualize successful outcomes.

Find something you can do better than anyone you know.

Accept life as it is.
Then work to make it the
way you want it to be.

You don't have to solve other people's problems.

Observe people who are successful at doing what you want to do. Then imitate them.

Look out for opportunity—and you'll find it everywhere!

All things being equal, choose the easy way.

Praise what you like about others; ignore what you don't.

Get *The Relaxation and Stress Reduction Workbook* and use it.

It's your life. Do what *you* want to do with it.

Let others know when you're angry with them, and why.

Have a first aid kit and let everybody know where it is.

Have more candlelight dinners.

Never go to bed mad.

If you don't know what you want, pretend a friend is in your shoes and ask yourself what the friend would want.

Take time to
laugh every day.

Accept whatever good
you are offered.

It's okay for you to change your mind.

You can control only
your own behavior.

Even a rainy day can be enjoyable.

The greatest secret of
women who win is persistence.

When you think about it,
everything is a miracle!

Always get enough sleep.

Focus on making your strengths even stronger, rather than on turning your weaknesses into strengths.

Remind yourself that you are a valuable, worthwhile human being.

You don't have to say it just
because you think it.

Do something you've
always wanted to do.

Think of how someone you
know yearns to be treated.
Treat them that way.

Shine, even if the sun doesn't.

Read an amusing book.

Call a friend to say hello.

List 3 qualities you like
about someone. Slip your
list into his or her jacket.

Make a donation to a good cause.

Cheer up someone who needs it.

Check in with your feelings now and then. Do it by sitting in a quiet place and asking yourself, "What am I feeling? Am I tired? Angry?" etc.

Feel the wind.

Pop some popcorn.

Tell more jokes.

Build a support system of friends.

Find work you like and consider worthwhile.

If you're not happy, take a day off and make concrete plans to change your life.

Hug 3 times a day.

Say "I love you" more often,
but only when you really mean it.

Wear #15 sun block.

Forgive others for past mistakes, and more importantly, forgive yourself.

Go somewhere you've never been.

Accept life as it is; don't hold out for it being as you think it should be.

When beginning friendships, start small. Acquaintances are more likely to agree to a chat over coffee than they are to dinner.

Temptation is easier to avoid
if you keep far away.

Simplify your life.

Don't blame your parents.
Take responsibility for
your own life.

Help a neighbor.

Give more than is expected.

Go for what you want.
You regret most those times
you don't try, not those
times you try and fail.

Write out your good qualities. Put
the list where you can see it often.

Never criticize anyone
in front of others.

Don't bother trying for
everybody's approval.
You'll never even come close.

Listen carefully, and you'll never be at a loss for words.

Ask questions from *The Book of Questions* to stimulate conversation.

Happiness is a do-it-yourself project.

Change is inevitable — so welcome it!

Thank people who help you.

Don't borrow unless you have to.

Be kind.

Feed the birds.

Take things step by step. It's easier to get to the 5th rung of a ladder after you've climbed the first 4.

Make people
more important
than possessions.

When you feel angry, cool down before you speak up.

Just because someone's angry doesn't mean they're right.

Read *How are Men Like Noodles?* to get a good laugh.

Visit a relative.

Go on a hike.

Introduce yourself to new
people at every opportunity.

Make a "To Do" list each day, and cross off each item as you complete it.

Plan for the future, then work towards making your plans a reality.

Surprise a friend with flowers.

Take time to relax.

Don't use drugs or alcohol to escape reality. It doesn't work and will cause you far more pain in the long run.

Read contracts at home, when you have time to think about them.

Get more massages.

True enlightenment is lightening up on yourself.

When looking for a man,
a job, or an apartment, ask
your friends to help.

Take a class in
French cooking.

Keep track of where your
money is going.

Help someone
who's too shy to ask.

Ask yourself what you would
do with your life if money were not
a consideration. Perhaps you can
find a way to do that now.

Eat more pasta and less meat.

Set aside time each day to do
with as *you* like.

Cut out articles you think
will interest others and
pass them along.

Buy something new every
time you go to the market.

Try out a new hairstyle.

Take low-impact aerobics.
Promise yourself a terrific reward if
you stick with it for a month.

Go to a fashion show.

Make friends with people who are already happy.

Be patient with yourself. Given enough time and effort, anyone can learn pretty much anything.

Don't be afraid to take risks.

Be honest with others

Be honest with yourself.

Be even more loving to
others when the world is
being cruel to you.

Find a way to serve others and your life will have meaning.

Set aside a Saturday
to do nothing.

When there's conflict, look first
to the role *you* play.

Love yourself.
And show it by treating
yourself with kindness.

Make friends with your neighbors.

Never put your life on hold.

Use your potential.
Just *having* a terrific potential
won't do you any good.

Let go of problems
you can't change.

Have close relationships, but
always keep some space for yourself.

Consider how your actions
will affect others.

Nike is right — "Just do it!"

Work towards improvement — not perfection.

Make the effort, even if you're not sure of the outcome.

Welcome everyone's success.

Judge others by their *actions*, not their words.

Good friendships take work.

Get specific about your goals.

Always have a short term and a long term goal to work towards.

Know that you are much *more* than just your looks.

Every once in a while,
spoil yourself.

The more effort you put out, the luckier you'll get.

Refuse to label yourself. Just because you have failed doesn't mean you are a failure. Just because you have acted shy in the past doesn't mean you can't change.

Balance your working time with play.

Sit up straight.

It's not your fault if
everything isn't right and
everyone isn't happy.

Make your home environment beautiful.

Eat whatever you want, but control how much of it you eat.

When you eat sweets, focus your *total* attention on the sensation. You'll be satisfied eating far less that way.

When you are dealt a bad hand, play it well.

Check out an audio book and listen to it while you drive, cook and walk.

Treat others as if they *already are* what you know they *can be.* They'll love you for it!

When you feel depressed, exercise, even if you don't want to.

If you're often depressed, read *Feeling Good* and *Control Your Depression*. They'll help you understand the thinking that makes you depressed so you can change it.

Don't waste time worrying about the future. Worry won't change a thing.

Approach every morning as a new chance.

Find a mentor.

Aim high.

Don't buy the biggest, buy the best.

Invite someone you disagree with to lunch. Find out why they think the way they do.

Before you can get what you want, you must decide what you want.

Share your dreams only with people who will cheer you on.

Hear others out completely before judging.

Be child*like*, not child*ish*.

Make it a point to think positive,
upbeat, and encouraging thoughts

The surest form of help
is *self*-help.

Visit someone who's lonely.

Respect everyone. Each person you meet is better than you at something and has a lesson to teach you.

Start tasks well before the deadline. You won't feel rushed — and that'll leave time later for having fun!

Give you bedroom a facelift, complete with new curtains, sheets, and a new bedspread.

If you can, buy it on special.

Give your mind a lift everyday by reading something inspiring.

Be good to yourself.

Find a way to exercise that you can enjoy, not just put up with.

Stop criticizing your body. Decide that as long as you exercise a reasonable amount and eat reasonably well, that's GOOD ENOUGH.

Have a movie night at your house, complete with popcorn and candy. Invite friends to join you.

If possible, never quit a job until you've already got another.

Send lots of postcards to keep in touch with friends and familly.

Watch more comedies.

Make friends with people who help you feel good about yourself.

You are where you are because you think what you think. If you don't like where you are, change your thinking.

Find a getaway where you can enjoy peace and quiet, perhaps a garden or a lake near you. Go there often.

Have another getaway, this one in your mind. Make it a nice place to visit when the going gets rough and you need some time out.

Put the past in the past.

When you're working towards
your goals, expect to make mistakes.

Give up trying to control others.

Do your share to save the planet.

Choose positive motivators.
For example, instead of eating low calorie foods because you're afraid of being fat, choose them because you want to be healthy and trim.

Don't compare yourself with others.

Go bicycle riding with a friend.

Start waking up half an hour early.
Use that time to go walking and hear
the birds sing. Or to do some stretching
exercises. Or to simply enjoy the quiet.
You won't miss the sleep and the time
will set a nice tone for the day.

If you do it, do it well.

Spend a weekend at a
spa being pampered.

Try a sport or game
you've never played.

Join a club made up of other
women who share at least one
of your interests.

When you feel anxious,
breathe deeply.

On the job, always dress
like the people the next step
or two up.

Begin with a sincere compliment
before giving criticism.

Always have enough gas
or money to get home.

To get to know someone, ask
about their childhood.

When you're trying something new,
recognize that mistakes and confusion
are part of the process.

Accept yourself as you are.

Live with passion.

Buy fresh flowers—just for you!

No matter the problem,
love is usually at least part
of the answer.

Eat a carrot or an apple before dinner and you'll feel full sooner.

Write friends' birthdays on your calendar or datebook and call them with congratulations.

Even if you're sure you're smarter, never let others know.

It costs less to learn from the mistakes of others than to learn by making them yourself.

When you're asked to guess someone's age, guess low.

When you're asked to guess how much something cost, guess high.

Balance work and play.

Adopt a "no knock" policy towards others. For 90 days, don't criticize anyone. It'll improve *all* your relationships.

If what you're doing isn't working, do something else.

Are you smiling?
Draw a picture of yourself.

Read *Balcony People*
to learn how to be an
"encourager" for others.

Promptly return
everything you borrow.

Sometimes, the best you can
do is to just hang in there.

Buy a terrific new
accessory every few months.

When negative things happen, find a positive way to respond.

When in doubt, add a little more postage.

When you're busy or enjoying a quiet time, let the machine answer the phone.

Vote.

Rest when your body
tells you to.

Get a guidebook and visit
everything within 75 miles
of your home.

When you make a mistake, laugh at yourself.

Experience different types of music now and then.

Don't ignore pain.
See a doctor.

If you want
things to happen,
work to make
them happen.

When you disagree, do it in
a way that isn't disagreeable.

Face life's difficulties and
responsibilities head on.
It's easier in the long run.

Don't try to be a Superwoman.
If you're too busy, hire help.

When you feel angry, pause
a moment before speaking.

Read *Your Erroneous Zones*
to help yourself build a life
that works.

Accept responsibility for your
part when things go wrong.

*Seek out the good
in every situation—
and you'll find it!*